THE LITTLE BOOK OF
MANIFESTATION

ASTRID CARVEL

Andrews McMeel
PUBLISHING®

Andrews McMeel Publishing
a division of Andrews McMeel Universal
1130 Walnut Street, Kansas City, Missouri 64106

www.andrewsmcmeel.com

23 24 25 26 27 SHO 10 9 8 7 6 5 4 3 2 1

ISBN: 978-1-5248-8023-1

Library of Congress Control Number: 2022937685

Text: Hannah Bowstead
Editor: Jean Lucas
Designer: Rhea Wyss
Production Editor: Elizabeth A. Garcia
Production Manager: Chadd Keim

ATTENTION: SCHOOLS AND BUSINESSES
Andrews McMeel books are available at quantity discounts with bulk purchase for educational, business, or sales promotional use. For information, please e-mail the Andrews McMeel Publishing Special Sales Department: specialsales@amuniversal.com.

CONTENTS

DISCLAIMER

The author and the publisher cannot accept responsibility for any misuse or misunderstanding of any information contained herein, or any loss, damage or injury, be it health, financial or otherwise, suffered by any individual or group acting upon or relying on information contained herein. None of the views or suggestions in this book is intended to replace medical opinion from a doctor who is familiar with your particular circumstances. If you have concerns about your health, please seek professional advice.

INTRODUCTION

Is it really true that you have the power to make your dreams a reality? Chances are, if you've picked up this book, you've already heard about the power of manifestation to land your dream career, find your soul mate, or improve your health and finances. And with a little know-how, and a healthy dose of focus and effort, manifestation can indeed help you achieve all that—and more. This book will be your guide to manifestation. In the following chapters, it will explain what manifesting is, delve into its history, and lay out everything you need to know to get started. It also provides a rich variety of manifestation techniques and practices to help you achieve your goals, as well as advice for keeping up the momentum once you get going. If you've never encountered manifestation before, or if you've heard about what it can do and are eager to learn more, this book will act as your companion as you begin a journey toward realizing your deepest desires. It's time to start changing your life.

CHAPTER ONE

WHAT IS MANIFESTATION?

Making your dreams come true and getting everything you want sounds great. But what actually is manifestation? How and why does it work? And what do you need to know to get started? The world of manifestation can seem confusing and overwhelming for beginners, with so many terms, tasks, and techniques, but this chapter will help you decode and understand all this. It covers the basics: the core beliefs and principles behind manifestation practice, the reasons these principles work the way they do, and how it all comes together to allow you to enact real change in your life.

WHAT DOES "MANIFESTATION" MEAN?

"Manifestation" can mean many different things to many different people, but a simple definition might be that it is the practice of bringing your aspirations into being through your thoughts and your energy. That's right: through manifestation, you have the power to make your dreams and desires real, whether it's success, money, or love that you seek. There are countless manifesting techniques, plenty of which we'll cover later in this book, but what they all have in common is the practice of focusing your thoughts and energy on a particular goal in order to make clear to the universe exactly what you want. With belief and effort, what you desire will find its way into your life, as long as you remain receptive. The practices and techniques of manifesting your goals are based on something called the law of attraction, which is the guiding principle of manifestation.

THE LAW OF ATTRACTION

There is a set of fundamental laws that govern the entire universe. For those who practice manifestation, the law of attraction is one such law. This law is the principle that we are able to attract into our lives whatever we focus our energy on. Think of your body like a magnet: if you focus on the positive energy within yourself, then you will be able to draw positive energy from the universe. Forget about the old saying "opposites attract"; with the law of attraction, it's the other way around. Like attracts like, positive energy attracts positive energy, and negative energy attracts negative energy. But don't worry—you're in control and you get to decide what to attract, or manifest, into your life. The law of attraction is what makes manifestation possible: the universe is ready to give you everything you want, if you are only ready and willing to attract it.

VIBRATION AND FREQUENCY

To understand the law of attraction better, it helps to explore the concepts of vibration and frequency. Everything in the universe, all the energy, is constantly moving. This is vibration. All this energy vibrates at different rates, and the rate at which something vibrates is its frequency. Something that is vibrating at a certain frequency has the power to attract other things vibrating at a similar frequency. This is the reason why, according to the law of attraction, "like energy" is attracted to "like energy." Our thoughts also have a vibrational frequency and so we are able to manifest, or attract, certain things into our reality by changing our frequency. If you surround yourself with feelings of anger and negativity, your vibrational frequency will lower and you will attract negative experiences. But if you focus on feelings of happiness and positivity, you can raise your frequency and will be able to manifest good things.

TRUST IN THE
POWER OF THE
UNIVERSE

VISUALIZATION

Once you understand that the universe is ready to give you what you want, you need to find a way of communicating your desires. Visualization is a core component of manifestation for this very reason. The techniques of visualization help you to picture, with precision and clarity, what you're trying to manifest. This heightens your focus and motivation to reach your goal, especially if you are able to visualize the emotions that will come with achieving it. Visualization can take the form of a physical vision board on which you collect pictures that represent your dream, or it can take place entirely in your mind. What's important is that you are truly able to picture yourself having already achieved your goal—what that looks, sounds, and feels like. This will raise your frequency, bringing your energy in line with the energy of whatever it is you want to attract into your life.

PUT IN THE HARD WORK

Manifestation isn't just about thinking and focusing hard on what you want. Unfortunately, you can't just sit back after visualization and expect change to happen instantly. You have to be prepared to put in the work and act on your desires. It helps to think of manifestation as a collaboration between you and the universe: you've told the universe precisely what you want and now you must work with it to achieve your goal. For example, someone wanting to manifest wealth might start researching possible side hustles or even ask for a pay raise at work. Throughout this process, it's important to remain receptive to opportunities that come your way. If you're trying to manifest a relationship and someone offers you tickets to an event, this could be the universe telling you that your soul mate is waiting for you there! Put in the effort, be open to change, and listen to the universe.

LIFE OPENS UP OPPORTUNITIES TO YOU, AND YOU EITHER TAKE THEM OR YOU STAY AFRAID OF TAKING THEM.

JIM CARREY

MAKE IT HAPPEN

You will find plenty of people who dismiss manifestation as make-believe or too good to be true. Many of these criticisms stem from the mistaken belief that manifestation is magic and will grant you infinite wishes at the snap of your fingers. This is a misunderstanding. The basic premise of manifestation—like attracts like— is something that is readily accepted by most people. If you are kind to someone, they are much more likely to be kind to you. It's as simple as that! In the same way, when you regularly think about and visualize your dream in a positive light, you will be more inspired and motivated to make it happen, as well as being more open to positive opportunities that come your way. Just remember: manifestation is a tool to help you reach success. It cannot solve all your problems overnight! But if you're willing to put in the time, commit your effort to it, and be patient, manifestation can take you to amazing places.

CHAPTER TWO:

A BRIEF HISTORY OF MANIFESTATION

The beliefs and techniques of manifestation have been shaped and influenced by a diverse range of thinkers across the years. The following pages chart the history of manifestation, from its origins in the nineteenth-century New Thought movement, through the development of the law of attraction, to the popularization and accessibility of manifestation in more recent times. This chapter also introduces a host of famous faces who attribute their success to manifestation, visualization, or the law of attraction. You'll gain a greater appreciation for the enduring power of manifestation, which has benefited so many lives throughout the centuries.

PHINEAS QUIMBY AND NEW THOUGHT

Manifestation and the law of attraction have their basis in the New Thought movement, which arose in the United States in the early nineteenth century. The spiritual successor of "ancient thought" from cultures including the ancient Greeks, Romans, Egyptians, Chinese, Hindus, and Buddhists, New Thought suggests that humans are inherently spiritual beings and we manifest our lives and experiences through our mental states. Many people consider the mesmerist (hypnotist) Phineas Quimby to be the founder of New Thought. Born in 1802, Quimby suffered from tuberculosis in his youth but noticed that brief periods of joy or excitement alleviated his symptoms. Later he became fascinated by the mind's ability to influence the body. He believed that the mind was the cause of illness and could therefore also be the cure, if the right mental state was achieved. This basic belief, although focused solely on illness and health, would develop over time into the principles of manifestation that we recognize today.

THE ORIGINS OF
THE LAW OF ATTRACTION

Although echoes of the law of attraction can be found throughout ancient teachings and the beginnings of the New Thought tradition, the principle would not be formally defined and developed until the second half of the nineteenth century. Many consider Prentice Mulford, a pivotal New Thought figure, to be the first person to explain the law of attraction and how it worked. Mulford's work, *Your Forces and How to Use Them*, published between 1886 and 1892, forms the basis of our modern understanding of the law of attraction, explaining clearly how our thoughts influence and define the world around us. Crucially, Mulford was also one of the first to expand these principles beyond the previous focus on physical health, arguing that the law of attraction could influence everything from life events and opportunities to material possessions and wealth.

THE 20TH CENTURY

Following in the footsteps of pioneers like Quimby and Mulford, an increasing number of thinkers and writers began expanding the principles of New Thought in the early 20th century. William Walker Atkinson, a businessman and attorney, suffered a physical and mental breakdown due to the stress of his working life. Attributing his recovery to the law of attraction, he found healing in the New Thought movement. He wrote around a hundred books about his experiences in the late 19th and early 20th centuries, believing willpower and concentration to be fundamental components of successful attraction. Another standout manifestation pioneer is Wallace Delois Wattles. He wrote the 1910 book *The Science of Getting Rich*, which played a crucial role in demystifying the law of attraction for a wider audience. Wattles expanded on Quimby's work on mental healing to demonstrate that the same principle applies to financial success, and he also promoted the technique of creative visualization, which remains core to manifestation practice today.

WHATEVER
THE MIND CAN
CONCEIVE
AND BELIEVE,
THE MIND CAN
ACHIEVE.

NAPOLEON HILL

MANIFESTATION DEMOCRATIZED

In 1937, another work was published that would be pivotal in expanding and popularizing the law of attraction and manifestation. *Think and Grow Rich* by Napoleon Hill defines a "Philosophy of Achievement," which states that anyone can manifest wealth and success through expectation, desire, and perseverance. It has sold over 15 million copies. The principles of manifestation were becoming more and more accessible, and this only continued as the 20th century progressed. In the 1980s, Jerry and Esther Hicks popularized the teaching that we are creators who can manifest our realities through our thoughts and attention. Around the same time, New Thought writer Louise Hay was encouraging the use of affirmations to achieve a positive mindset and influence reality, primarily in her phenomenally successful book *You Can Heal Your Life* (1984). The message was becoming clearer: success is not just for the privileged but can be achieved by anyone through the power of thoughts and energy.

THE SECRET

Many contemporary manifestation practices have arisen from a pivotal work from 2006: *The Secret* by Rhonda Byrne. This documentary film, and the accompanying book published in the same year, features interviews and testimonies from some of the foremost figures in the movement at that time. Building on existing works, *The Secret* lays out the law of attraction in clear terms and explains how it works to enable us to create the lives we want. Byrne outlines a three-step process for manifesting your deepest desires—"ask, believe, receive"—and emphasizes the importance of visualization and gratitude as fundamental aspects of manifesting through the law of attraction. Many of the key ideas in *The Secret*, such as "ask, believe, receive," visualization, and gratitude, have become core components of modern manifestation practices and techniques.

FAMOUS SUCCESSES

Since *The Secret*, manifestation has grown in fame and popularity, with many celebrities either expressing themselves as manifestation believers or aligning with the core principles of the law of attraction.

Oprah Winfrey is one of manifestation's most famous followers. She spoke in an interview in May 2007 about how she believes she manifested her role in the film *The Color Purple*. She is a vocal advocate for the power of manifestation, having frequently endorsed manifestation books and figures on her show, website, and beyond.

Jim Carrey is another firm believer in manifestation. On *The Oprah Winfrey Show* in February 1997, he explained that, prior to being famous, every day he visualized having a prosperous acting career, even writing himself a check for $10 million in the knowledge that he would one day earn it. And guess what? He did!

Will Smith credits his belief that we are who we choose to be as the reason for his success, saying that if you truly believe in yourself, the universe will allow you to achieve your goal.

Arnold Schwarzenegger has spoken about how he used visualization to attract success into both his bodybuilding and acting careers. He knew he would win the Mr. Universe bodybuilding title and find fame as an actor, because visualizing these outcomes had removed all his doubt.

Lady Gaga used positive affirmations to help make her dream of being a successful musician a reality. She truly believed that one day her affirmations would come true—and she was right.

These are just a few of the famous faces that have used manifestation techniques and practices to attract positive change into their lives and to achieve great things.

GOOD THINGS
ARE HEADING
YOUR WAY—GET
READY!

MANIFESTATION TODAY

Although *The Secret* helped to popularize manifestation, the practice is now reaching bigger and broader audiences than ever before thanks to social media. Throughout the past couple of years, interest in manifestation and associated practices like visualization has boomed on sites such as Instagram and Twitter. TikTok in particular has provided a huge platform for discussing manifestation and sharing tips, with posts tagged #manifestation or #lawofattraction garnering billions of views. The topic's popularity soared throughout the coronavirus pandemic lockdowns, perhaps because of an increased need for positive energy and looking forward or because many became more focused on introspection and self-care. Indeed, many contemporary manifestation followers view it as part of wellness and self-care, due to its focus on positive thinking as well as the calming, even therapeutic rituals of manifestation practice. One thing is for sure: manifestation techniques have never before been so readily accessible, making today the perfect time to give them a try.

CHAPTER THREE:

THE BASICS OF MANIFESTATION

Now that you know about the law of attraction, its history, and how it works to help you achieve your goals, it's time to start thinking about how to practice manifestation. You might be wondering what happens in a manifestation session, what some of the words and phrases thrown around actually mean, or what tools, both material and mental, you need in order to manifest effectively. Manifestation is a big topic, and it's natural to feel somewhat overwhelmed by all this new information. But don't worry. This chapter breaks down and explains these key basics of manifestation so that you can begin practicing with confidence.

BASIC MANIFESTATION STEPS

If you're a beginner, it might help to think of a manifestation (that is, the act of manifesting one individual thing) in five main steps:

1. Choose what you want to manifest

2. Visualize and/or script your desires

3. Identify and remove obstacles (also known as manifestation blocks)

4. Take action

5. Acknowledge and be grateful

These steps and how to carry them out will be covered in much more detail in the following chapter, so don't be alarmed if you're confused. Usually a manifestation session will be concerned with step two: visualization and scripting. You will already have chosen what to manifest when you sit down for a session, and during this time you will visualize your goal and send a strong message to the universe using any number of techniques. Over time you will develop your own personal preferences, such as using sounds, scents, candles, or other aids. And that's all there is to it.

YOU HAVE
THE POWER
TO MAKE YOUR
DREAMS A
REALITY

MANIFESTATION JARGON-BUSTER

Practitioners of manifestation often use many different words and terms, and it isn't always obvious what they mean. This list of commonly used terms will help.

- **"Scripting"** is any manifestation technique that involves writing down your manifestations. It's very popular on social media. Scripting methods mostly require you to write in the present or past tense, as though you have already achieved your desired outcome.

- **"Frequency"** is the rate at which energy vibrates, but the term is also used to refer to sounds that have a specific frequency to aid manifestation. For example, the "love" frequency is 528 Hz, and listening to this while manifesting a relationship will help send a stronger message to the universe.

- **"Creative visualization"** is the process of conjuring strong mental imagery of what you're trying to manifest, including what it looks, sounds, smells, tastes, and feels like. This helps you experience the emotions of having achieved your goal, bringing your frequency and energy in line with what you're trying to attract.

- **"Affirmations"** are short, positive mantras that you can repeat to yourself in order to reprogram your subconscious and gradually change your mindset.

- **"Manifestation blocks"** refer to anything that prevents or obstructs you from manifesting successfully. They include (but are not limited to) negative beliefs or mindset, toxic people and relationships, wrong timing, and bad habits.

- An **"angel number"** is a set of repeated digits (for example 111, 222, or 333) that keeps appearing in a person's life. If you keep noticing the same number over and over, this could be your angel number. The different numbers mean different things, but they are all messages from the universe, like an angel watching over or guiding you.

- **"Ask, believe, receive"** is a phrase popularized in *The Secret* that is shorthand for the process of attracting your desires through manifestation and the law of attraction.

- **"Ask the universe"** refers to the first step of "ask, believe, receive": sending a clear message, through visualization, scripting, or another method, to the universe about what you want.

ASK FOR WHAT
YOU WANT AND
BE PREPARED
TO GET IT.

MAYA ANGELOU

WHAT YOU'LL NEED

You don't need much to begin manifesting—just a quiet space for carrying out your sessions. But as manifestation becomes an integrated aspect of your life, you might want to invest in some supplies.

- **Journal and pen:** These are essential for any scripting technique, as you are required to write your manifestations down. Choose a journal that fills you with positive energy and inspiration, or decorate it yourself.
- **Candles and scents:** These can aid with your energy and focus, as well as creating an attractive manifestation space where you want to spend time.
- **Headphones or speakers:** If you use sound frequencies during your manifestation sessions, you'll need some way of playing them. Pick headphones for true immersion.
- **Crystals:** The vibrations of different crystals can amplify your own energy, making them excellent aids for manifestation.
- **Sage:** Burning a sage smudge stick cleanses your home of negative energy. Just make sure you keep the windows open, and don't burn sage if you have children or pets in the house, as inhaling the smoke can be harmful if not done correctly.

THE RIGHT MINDSET

It's not just about getting some cool gear (although we all still love that back-to-school new-stationery feeling); what's more important for successful manifestation is cultivating the right mindset. Ensure that you are working to foster these attributes as you embark on your manifestation journey.

- **Positivity:** It's crucial that you maintain a positive mindset when you are manifesting, and throughout your life in general. Remember, positive things are attracted to positive energy, and negative things to negative energy. Make sure that you're only welcoming good things into your life by thinking and behaving positively. Good vibes only!

- **Belief:** If you don't truly believe that you have the power to manifest your reality, then it won't work! That's because not having faith in what you're doing will lower your vibration, meaning your energy isn't aligned with the energy of what you're trying to manifest. So it's worth investing some time to ensure that low confidence, self-doubt, or skepticism don't stand between you and achieving your goals.

- **Patience:** If you're manifesting a career or your soul mate, don't be surprised when it doesn't happen instantly. While it is possible to manifest some smaller things (a phone call, a $50 gift) overnight, achieving your biggest goals through manifestation takes time, so you need to be patient. Look out for signs from the universe and be ready to jump on opportunities that might bring you closer to your goal.

- **Willingness:** To manifest anything, you must be willing to put in the effort and take action. The universe has heard you and is working for you, but you have to hold up your side of the bargain. If you're not prepared to work hard for your dreams, you're saying that you don't really want them that much. So why should the universe help you? You should also be willing to accept gifts from the universe, even if they are not *quite* what you were expecting. Trust and show willingness, and you will soon be on the path to success.

CHAPTER FOUR:

MANIFESTATION PRACTICES

It's time to start manifesting! The previous chapter explained how manifestation can be broken into five stages: choosing what to manifest, visualization or scripting, removing manifestation blocks, taking action, and showing gratitude. This chapter will explore in greater depth the first three of these steps, providing tips for selecting your manifestations, examples of visualization and scripting methods to suit a range of abilities and tastes, and advice for overcoming some of the most common manifestation blocks. By the chapter's end, you'll be ready to put it all into practice and start attracting your biggest dreams into your life.

CHOOSE WHAT TO MANIFEST

You might already know what it is you want to manifest into your life, or you might have some idea but be a bit hazy on the details, or you might not have the first clue! In any case, the following tips and advice will help you pinpoint what sort of manifestation will be authentic to yourself and your life and will be beneficial to you and the people around you. So if you think you've got it all figured out, or you're terrified because everyone else seems to have it all figured out, these ideas will be of use and benefit to you.

IF MONEY WERE NO OBJECT

It can be overwhelming to think about what your deepest desires truly are. It's easy to find yourself limiting your dreams because of other people's expectations about what success looks like or because of your own beliefs about what's normal and acceptable within your social circles. But with the law of attraction, anything is possible if you're prepared to put in the hard work. Think of it this way: if money were no object, what are the five things that you would most want to do with your life? Would you still want to work, and, if so, doing what? Would you want to travel? Spend more time with your loved ones? Or develop your favorite hobby or passion? This will help you focus on what *your* goals are rather than what society thinks you should be aiming toward. This way, you'll create manifestations based on your authentic self, and you'll be much more likely to find success with the law of attraction.

DON'T BE AFRAID

Dreaming big is scary. Most people stop themselves from thinking or dreaming about what it is they truly want from life because they are afraid that they won't achieve it and will be disappointed. They believe that it is better to stay confined in a life, relationship, or job that's just *OK*, rather than take a big leap and run the risk of failure and embarrassment. This is why some people will try and tell you that your dreams are "unrealistic." But don't listen! Anything you put your mind to and work hard toward, you can achieve. So don't be afraid to dream big and ask the universe for whatever you really desire, rather than half-heartedly manifesting something that you only *sort of* want because you think it's more reasonable. It might be hard at first to believe deeply in your own power and worthiness, and big dreams always require time and patience, but it will be more than worth it when you have achieved everything you dreamed of!

ALWAYS GO
WITH YOUR
PASSIONS.
NEVER ASK
YOURSELF IF
IT'S REALISTIC
OR NOT.

DEEPAK CHOPRA

ASKING THE RIGHT QUESTIONS

However much we want, we can't just manifest anything—what you're asking for has to be right for you and other people. You really shouldn't try to manifest anything that will bring harm to you or anyone else. So it makes sense to think carefully about what you're going to manifest. To help you decide if your manifestation is going to be the right thing for you, ask yourself the following questions:

- Do I really want this?

- How will having this benefit me?

- When I think about having this, does it feel right?

- Will this be helpful or harmful to me and others?

Thinking your manifestation through in this way will help ensure it's something that will bring you joy and fulfillment and may even prevent you from manifesting something with unintended consequences. After all, the old saying "Be careful what you wish for" applies to manifestation too!

WHAT IF YOU DON'T KNOW?

It's all well and good if you've known since the age of 10 that you want to be a vet and have three children. But plenty of people don't have any idea what to manifest. So, don't panic if you're not sure whether your true calling is to be a lawyer or a barista—there are three things to remember. One: it's OK not to know. In fact, it's more fun! Think of this as an opportunity to learn about yourself and explore new opportunities and experiences. Two: you don't have to manifest defined, physical things. Think about qualities rather than specific things that you'd like to attract into your life, such as confidence, a creative work environment, or a reduction in your stress levels. Then be on the lookout for signs from the universe! And three: you can change your mind! Once you've started manifesting, nothing is set in stone, so you are free to adapt your manifestations based on your new experiences, emotions, and gut instincts.

VISUALIZATION AND SCRIPTING

This is the bread and butter of manifestation. In the following pages you'll find plenty of methods and techniques for your manifestation sessions, as well as tips for making it work. These methods are roughly divided into two types: visualization and scripting. Visualization is a powerful tool frequently used by athletes as a "dress rehearsal" for big performances and is used in manifestation to conjure a detailed image and send a strong message to the universe. Scripting methods involve writing or journaling your manifestations in various ways. There's something here to suit everyone, so you'll be manifesting in no time.

IF YOU
BELIEVE IT,
YOU CAN DO IT

MAKING A VISION BOARD

Visualization is a key component of many manifestation practices, but it can be a bit overwhelming for a beginner. You might be wondering what you're actually supposed to *do* or think when you're visualizing. If you are a bit unsure about visualization, then creating a vision board is a good place to start. A vision board is a bit like a mood board that's filled with images and items that represent or align closely with your chosen manifestation. The process of creating a vision board helps with manifestation, but the board can also be used afterward during visualization sessions. It's the perfect way to get started with visualization as it's a physical object that you can focus on, meaning you don't have to be so worried about drifting away in your thoughts and losing focus. Vision boards are also long-lasting, acting as a colorful and continued source of inspiration and encouragement as you work toward your goal. Plus, they're really fun to create!

You'll need a big piece of poster board as the base (the bigger the better!), scissors, and glue. Set aside a few hours and make your space cozy and calming. Collect as many magazines, catalogs, or decorative papers as you can find, and search them for images that represent your manifestation, or that inspire you or speak to you during this process. Cut these out. You could also use wrapping paper, wallpaper, stickers, postcards, fabric, leaves and flowers, or anything else you can find. Be imaginative! Once you've collected all your images, arrange them on your poster board and, once you're happy with your layout, glue them down. Decorate or fill any gaps in your board with markers and paint, ribbons, sequins, or colorful tape. Add key words or phrases that link to your manifestation as you see fit. Keep your vision board under some heavy books to ensure it dries flat, then hang it up where you'll see it every day, as a reminder of what you're going to achieve.

USING YOUR VISION BOARD

Now you know how to create a vision board, but that's only one half of the story. The mindset you adopt while creating your board is as crucial as the images you choose to adorn it with. As you select images, words, and motifs for your vision board, be mindful of how you're feeling. Imagine that you have already achieved what you're trying to manifest, and focus on the emotions and sensations of that moment. Use these emotions to guide you in picking the images. If you're creating a vision board for your dream vacation, don't just choose images of sunbathers on a beach but consider certain colors and patterns that express the emotions you're imagining. This might include images that seem unconnected at first, but if they're resonating with you in the moment, add them to your board. Focusing on the sensations of achieving your goal as you create your vision board is, in itself, a visualization session.

Once your vision board is completed and on display somewhere prominent, it's time to start using it to guide you during visualization sessions. Simply having the board on display will help your subconscious align with your goal every time you see it, but the board can also be used to aid a more in-depth visualization. Sit facing your vision board and make your space conducive to visualization, using music, frequencies, scents, or candles. Using one of the visualization techniques in this chapter to help you if you wish, begin to imagine yourself having achieved your goal. Focus on the images and words on your vision board to help you picture the sights, sounds, and sensations of the scene. Remember the emotions each image inspired in you—why did you choose them? If any specific image seems to be calling you, allow your energy to settle on it for a time. Finally, repeat any words or affirmations on your board to bring your visualization to a close.

TIP: VISION BOARDS ON THE GO

A vision board doesn't just have to be a giant poster hanging on your wall. One of the key functions of vision boards is acting as a daily reminder of where you're headed, so try one of these ideas for creating a smaller, more portable (and more private) version.

- Create a vision board on the first page of your diary, daily planner, or journal.

- If you're studying, make a letter-size vision board and put it into one of your ring binders.

- Use the cover of your manifestation journal as a blank canvas for vision boarding.

- Create a virtual vision board using a site or app like Pinterest, so you always have it on hand on your phone or laptop.

- Use your virtual vision board (or take a picture of your physical board) as your phone's background or lock screen.

I BELIEVE
THAT I CAN
CREATE
WHATEVER
I WANT TO
CREATE.

WILL SMITH

BASIC CREATIVE VISUALIZATION

If you've tried vision boards and you want to move on, or they're not for you, give creative visualization a try. Creative visualization is, in essence, the process of conjuring powerful images of what you're trying to manifest, in order to gain the emotions and the energy needed to attract that desire. It can take many different forms, but the following steps will give you a basic overview of a simple creative visualization session, which you can then tailor to your own tastes and requirements. Technically, the only equipment you'll need is your brain, but additional supplies like music and frequencies, scents, and crystals can help create an environment that's conducive to effective visualization. Set aside 15 to 20 minutes each day, preferably at the same time, such as before bed, and make sure you won't be distracted. Then you're good to go! When done regularly, creative visualization can be an immensely powerful tool for reframing your mindset, inspiring confidence and self-belief, and empowering you to achieve anything.

Begin your visualization session with a brief meditation. Spend a few minutes focusing on your breathing, or use one of the meditation tips in this book. Once you have reached a state of peace, begin conjuring an image of the moment of achieving your goal. Spend time creating all the details of the scene: What can you see and hear? What physical sensations can you feel? What are you wearing? Who is present and what are they doing or saying? Immerse yourself in this image, making it as vivid as you can and absorbing all its intricacies. Now, focus on how you're feeling in this scene. Are you happy, proud, excited, or reassured? Hold on to these emotions as you slowly return to your present reality and your visualization session is complete. Throughout your daily life, allow the emotions you experienced during your visualization to shape your behavior and actions. This way, your energy will come into alignment with the energy of what you're trying to attract.

WRITE YOURSELF A CHECK

This could also be called the "Jim Carrey method," as it's one of the visualization techniques he used to manifest his success. It's suitable if you're trying to manifest money, wealth, or, in some cases, success (success isn't always tied to finances), and it's very simple. Write out a check (or an IOU if you don't have a checkbook) addressed to yourself and dated to whenever in the future you want to have earned the money by. For example, if you want to receive $50,000 by the time you turn 30, write out the check dated to whenever your 30th birthday will be. Keep your check somewhere close where you will see it often, such as your bedside table, or you can have it framed and hang it on your wall. The constant reminder of your future wealth will help keep your energy high and your motivation on track so you work hard.

VISUALIZATION TRIGGERS

You know how the faint smell of a particular food brings back a powerful memory of that vacation you had 10 years ago? Well, you can harness this power to your advantage with your visualization. Creating a sensory trigger that's connected to your visualization can help you perform and achieve when needed. During each visualization session, try listening to a particular piece of music or playlist or lighting a candle with a specific scent (one you're unlikely to smell anywhere else). Your brain will connect that music or smell with the emotions you're feeling during your visualization. Then, when you need to write that job application, go on that run, or get ready for that date, listen to the same music or light your candle again. The positive emotions of your visualization will come flooding back, and you'll be filled with positive energy and the motivation to go out and smash it!

TIP: SETTING THE MOOD

It's really important to enter into a manifestation session with the right mindset, especially if you're trying to introduce visualization or scripting methods into your daily routine. It's worth taking a little time before your daily session to set the mood and allow yourself to enter a state of receptiveness and calm. This can be done in any number of ways. You could have a relaxing hot bath, listen to some chilled-out instrumental music, go for a short walk in nature, or do 10 minutes of a repetitive craft like knitting. The good news is that all of these ideas can form part of your self-care routine, something that is really important not just for your own health and well-being but also for successful manifestation. Choose one that appeals to you or mix it up each day, and you'll soon find that your manifestation sessions run smoothly and are more effective.

IF YOU WANT
TO FIND THE
SECRETS OF
THE UNIVERSE,
THINK IN TERMS
OF ENERGY,
FREQUENCY, AND
VIBRATION.

NIKOLA TESLA

THE 3-6-9 METHOD

This is one of the most straightforward and popular scripting techniques out there. It's based on the idea that the numbers 3, 6, and 9 are spiritually significant and are the keys to the universe—a belief purportedly held by the inventor Nikola Tesla. These three numbers are mathematically important for a number of reasons, but they have broader meanings as well. For example, some believe that the number 3 represents energy, 6 represents frequency, and 9 represents vibration. Combining the three numbers creates the ideal state for manifestation: by writing our intentions and manifestations three, six, or nine times, we have a greater chance of connecting with the universe and attracting what we desire. This is why the 3-6-9 method is practiced by so many. It's also simple and easy to build into a busy daily routine, making it perfect for first-time manifestors.

You must first come up with a short affirmation that tells the universe what it is you want. Remember to phrase this in the present or past tense, as though you have already achieved your desire and are thanking the universe ("I am so grateful that I am on vacation in Tokyo"). Once you have your sentence, write it into your manifestation journal three times as soon as you wake up in the morning. Write it into your journal six times at lunchtime or in the afternoon. Finally, write it nine times just before you go to bed. Do this each day for 33 days and remember to combine it with positive action. What you are manifesting might happen before the 33 days are up, in which case you don't need to carry on. But don't panic if it hasn't happened by the end of the 33 days—sometimes the universe needs a little more time before the results start to show.

THE 3-6-9 METHOD—ALTERNATIVE

This is a variation of the 3-6-9 method covered previously. It's based on the same principle that the numbers 3, 6, and 9 are significant to the universe, but the application of the method is a little different. This 3-6-9 method is best used if you're trying to manifest an action or response from a specific person, such as a phone call or even an emotion. Just remember to be careful when asking the universe to influence people's thoughts and feelings. If your intentions or the expected outcome aren't positive for both you and the person involved, the universe is likely to refuse your request! However, this method can also work if you're trying to manifest an object or something material, such as money or a new car. Just substitute the name of the object for the person's name in the steps that follow.

Make sure you're in the right headspace before you begin—you can meditate or cleanse your space if this helps. The first step is to write the name of the person into your manifestation journal three times. Next, write your intention for what you want to happen into your journal six times (for example, "X and I have reconnected"). Finally, write out nine times the specific action you want the person to take (for example, "X called me and asked me out for dinner"). Some people say that it helps them if they write down the name in the morning, the intention in the afternoon, and the action in the evening, but you can also carry out all three steps in one sitting. Choose whichever is best suited to you and your daily schedule. You can repeat this every day for either 21 days (three weeks) or 30 days, or you can carry on every day until your manifestation comes true!

THE 55 × 5 METHOD

This method is similar to other scripting methods but is best suited if you have room in your schedule for a slightly longer manifestation session each day. This method also takes place over a shorter time period than other methods (only five days), so it's an excellent choice if you want results quickly or if there's a specific event or deadline that you're working toward. But because of the short timescale, make sure that what you're manifesting is reasonable and appropriate. Requesting that the universe deliver your true soul mate or a lifetime of wealth in five days, while technically possible, is a big ask! Be realistic and stay proportional to the time frame. Instead of asking for your soul mate or untold riches, ask for a promising date or a new moneymaking opportunity. This method often works best if you're only manifesting one thing at a time; that way, you can focus all your energy on that one thing for the duration of the five days.

Choose what to manifest and create an affirmation based on it, making sure it is clear and concise. Pick a time during your day when you can sit down in peace and truly focus on your manifestation and try to keep this time consistent across the five days. Open your manifestation journal and write your manifestation 55 times. It helps to mark out the 55th line in your journal before you begin, so that you're focusing on the manifestation rather than the counting! As you write, visualize the sensations and emotions of having attained your desire, and try not to let your mind wander. This process can take some time, so try listening to a frequency that aligns with your chosen manifestation to aid your focus and energy. Carry out this session for five days in a row, then hand your manifestation over to the universe and see what happens!

THE PILLOW METHOD

The two most important and influential times of the day for manifesting are first thing in the morning as we wake up and last thing at night before we go to sleep. The pillow method utilizes these transitional periods to create a technique for manifesting that is simple yet effective. There are a few reasons why the method works so well. It allows the last thought you have before going to bed to be full of positive energy (this has the delightful side effect of allowing you to wake up inspired and hopeful the following morning). It can help to rewrite your subconscious thought processes and programming during the liminal state of falling asleep. And entering the calm and relaxation of dreamland allows you to release any doubts or reservations you might be experiencing about your manifestation while letting the intention remain. This method is easy for beginners, doesn't take up a lot of time, and doesn't require any special supplies, so you can try it out tonight.

For this method, you only need a piece of paper and a pen (and a pillow, of course). Write out your manifestation on the paper. You won't be writing this out multiple times, so feel free to go into a bit more detail about what it is you're trying to manifest. What does it look, sound, and feel like? What attributes and details does this thing, person, or event have? And, most importantly, how do you feel about it? Be as specific as you like. Just before you go to bed, place the paper under your pillow and sleep on it—literally! The following morning, take the paper out from under your pillow. If you have a crystal, you can place the paper underneath it for the duration of the day to keep the paper's energy high. Then, simply place it back under your pillow as you go to bed the following night. Keep this up until your manifestation is successful.

OPEN
YOURSELF
UP TO
ABUNDANCE

TIP: MAKING SPACE

Creating a dedicated space for your manifestation practice that is full of high energy is a good way to increase the effectiveness of your manifestations. Choose a corner somewhere in your home where you can feel relaxed, like your bedroom. Create an armchair out of floor cushions, set up some mood lighting, and make sure you have a small table or shelf for your manifestation journal and tools. Add items to your space that represent you: if you love traveling, put up a map of the world on the wall; or if you love reading, place some of your most inspiring books on a shelf. Make the space nice and cozy. Add fairy lights, drapes, speakers for music, and a throw or two. Make it somewhere you want to spend your time. Invest in some crystals to amplify the energy of the space. Clear quartz is a good choice for a crystal newbie—it's believed to boost energy and aid focus. Finally, make sure to keep your manifestation corner clean and uncluttered!

A LETTER FROM FUTURE YOU

This technique is the perfect crossover between visualizing and scripting. If you're having trouble focusing your thoughts and energy during visualization sessions, or if you find yourself unenthusiastic about writing the same affirmation over and over again, this might be the perfect alternative for you to try. The basic idea is to imagine that you are at a set amount of time in the future, having achieved your manifestations, and to write a letter to your past self (that is, the you of right now) telling you all about it. The letter can be as long or as short as you like, so this technique can be tailored to a busy schedule or a free afternoon. Imagining what your future self would say is a powerful visualization technique—but you won't even realize you're visualizing! And the act of writing it all down solidifies your manifestation and sends a clear and precise message to the universe.

Ensure your mind is relaxed and open. Imagine that you have achieved your manifestation goal, and consider whether this is six months, one year, or five years from now. Take some writing paper and a pen and compose a letter to yourself from the future. Begin describing what your new life is like now that your manifestation has come into being. Tell your past self what you have achieved and how you did it. Add details about your now-real manifestation—for example, if you're writing about a new job, describe what your desk space looks like or what your daily routine is. Write down how all this makes you feel, as well as the best things about your new life. When you've signed off, seal the letter in an envelope. You can choose to write the future date on the front and open your letter once that date arrives, or you can decide never to read it—the act of writing the letter is powerful enough.

MANIFESTATION BOX

This technique is another crossover between visualization and scripting. It's reminiscent of creating a vision board in the sense that you're collecting physical things that represent or inspire your manifestation, but it can also incorporate scripting and journaling elements as well. And just like a vision board, it's perfect if you're more creatively minded or find it easier working with physical objects rather than imagining everything. A manifestation box is ideal if you find yourself a little overwhelmed by some of the more involved and lengthy visualization and scripting techniques, or if you simply want to let go of your manifestation and allow the universe to work its magic in its own time. Creating your manifestation box will only need to be done once per manifestation, but you can reuse the same box and fill it with different contents for more manifestations in the future.

Find a suitable box—this could be a shoebox, storage box, or jewelry box. If you like, you can decorate your box with papers, paints, or stickers, so that it inspires joy (this could help raise your energy as you fill the box). Collect items that resonate with your manifestation. These might be pictures, photos, quotes, affirmations, trinkets, or souvenirs that symbolize your desire or evoke powerful positive memories and emotions. For example, if you're trying to manifest success as an author, you could put your favorite pen or a novel that inspires you into your box. Now it's time to script your manifestation. You could write a diary entry, a letter to a relative, or use another of the scripting methods in this book. Seal your script in an envelope and place it into the box along with the other objects. Close the lid and place your box on a windowsill during the full moon, as this is a time of heightened natural energy. Place your box on the windowsill every full moon until your manifestation happens!

SCRIPT YOUR DAY

Most of these visualization and scripting techniques have focused on the big stuff: how to manifest your dream career, home, soul mate, or wealth. But you can also use scripting to manifest the little daily wins. In fact, doing this is likely to help you greatly as you work toward your longer-term goals. Scripting the day ahead can help you stay grounded in the present moment and keep you enthusiastic about taking the little steps toward your bigger goals. That perfect vacation might seem so far away that it's difficult to get excited about being there, and before long you start to feel disheartened and procrastination creeps in! If this sounds like you, try introducing daily scripting into your morning routine. Staying focused on the next step will help prevent you getting overwhelmed by your goals and will instead make them feel more attainable. You'll be more motivated and your energy will be consistently raised, helping the law of attraction to bring your goal within your reach much faster.

Carry out this technique as part of your morning routine. Take your manifestation journal and imagine you're writing a diary entry at the end of that day. What did you accomplish that day? What positive things happened, what things in particular are you thankful for, and how are you feeling? Go into as much detail about the events of the day as you like, focusing in particular on the little steps you took that brought you closer to your long-term goals. Now, as you go through your day, you can use your diary entry like a blueprint for the day's activities. You know that you'll be able to achieve what you set out to do, as you've already done it once (in your head). Plus, as motivation, you can call upon the emotions and feelings of accomplishment that you experienced when writing the diary entry. At the end of the day, read your diary entry back and reflect on the day's successes. Then start getting excited about tomorrow!

JOURNAL YOUR DREAMS

This chapter has already covered many techniques that make use of your manifestation journal, but there is no reason why you can't also sit down for a dedicated journaling session when the mood takes you. Try out some of these journaling prompts to get you started.

- Write down five of your biggest, toughest life goals. For each goal, write down three small steps that you could take today or this week.

- Write 10 things that you love about yourself and 10 things that you are looking for in your ideal partner.

- Write a letter to your best friend or sibling to tell them about an amazing date you just had or the fantastic opportunity you've just been offered.

- Write a day-in-the-life about yourself in your dream job. What are you getting up to and what are your work environment and colleagues like?

- Describe taking a tour through the perfect home that you've just bought.

- How important are love, money, work, friendships, or success to you? Which is the most important thing in your life?

- Write down the first five negative or self-limiting thoughts that you have. Find a way to flip them into something positive and self-affirming.

- Write a postcard home from your dream vacation location. Where are you and what are you up to?

- Think of a few celebrities or people known to you who have achieved great things. In what three ways can you emulate each of them?

- Write down 10 great things that you have accomplished in the past year.

TIP: COMING UP WITH SCRIPTING AFFIRMATIONS

It can be tricky to know how to phrase your affirmation in scripting techniques. Firstly, it doesn't need to be long and complicated; in fact, the opposite applies. According to Esther Hicks' Abraham-Hicks method, the process of manifestation begins after only 17 seconds, so try coming up with an affirmation that takes roughly 17 seconds to write. A shorter affirmation will also save your hands if you have to write it out dozens of times! Secondly, be specific. There's no point asking for "a job" if what you really want is a career in a specific industry. Don't be afraid to send the universe a clear message! And lastly, remember to phrase your affirmation in the present or past tense. Imagine what you will be saying and feeling once you have achieved your goal, and use that as a starting point. For example: "I am in a loving and fulfilling relationship" or "I am so grateful that I was offered a new job in journalism."

DON'T BE AFRAID
TO ASK THE
UNIVERSE—IT'S
LISTENING

MEDITATION FOR MANIFESTATION

Meditation is an excellent way of attaining a calm, focused mindset throughout your daily life. It's also perfect for entering into the right headspace for a manifestation session, so if you often find yourself getting distracted or losing focus during your manifestation sessions, try one of these simple meditations before you begin. For each meditation, find somewhere peaceful and sit or lie in a comfortable, relaxed position.

- Close your eyes. Breathe in through your nose for four seconds, hold this breath for a further seven seconds, then breathe out through your mouth slowly for eight seconds. Repeat this five times.

- Take notice of the space around you. Focus on five things you can see, four things you can hear, three things you can touch, two things you can smell, and one thing you can taste.

- Spend a few minutes paying close attention to the sensations and feelings of your body. Can you feel the fabric of your clothes against your skin? The carpet or floor underneath you? Or the tickle of hair brushing against your face?

- Starting with your feet and working your way up to your face, tense each group of muscles for 10 seconds, then release, focusing on how each area feels when it is totally relaxed.

- Choose an object, such as a flower or candle, and place it in front of you; spend a few minutes focusing on all its details, such as what it smells or might feel like.

- Place one hand on your belly, then slowly breathe in through your nose for a count of six and out through your nose for a count of six. Feel your diaphragm inflating so that your belly rises and pushes against your hand. Do this for two minutes.

AFFIRMATION STATION

Affirmations are an amazing tool for quickly boosting your energy's vibration throughout your day. You could say a few each morning as you wake up, each night before you sleep, as you begin your manifestation session, or whenever you need a little pick-me-up or burst of positivity. Here are some examples to get you started, but feel free to come up with ones that are personal and meaningful to you.

- I am strong and confident.

- Abundance is heading my way.

- I deserve happiness and success.

- I can achieve anything.

- Everything I desire will come to me.

EVERY SINGLE
SECOND IS AN
OPPORTUNITY
TO CHANGE
YOUR LIFE.

RHONDA BYRNE

FREQUENCIES

Listening to certain sound frequencies that align with the vibrational frequency of what you're trying to manifest can have a big impact on your manifestations. Here are a set of nine frequencies (often called the Solfeggio Frequencies) and their associated attributes. Pick whichever fits your manifestation best, then search for that frequency on YouTube or Spotify.

- **174 Hz** – for relieving pain and stress. Use it to bring calm to your manifestation session after a hectic or difficult day.

- **285 Hz** – for healing minor physical injuries. This frequency can be used to help soothe smaller physical ailments or rejuvenate the body.

- **396 Hz** – for removing negative thoughts, fear, guilt, and self-doubt. Use this one if you're struggling with a negative mindset that's blocking your manifestations.

- **417 Hz** – for initiating change. This frequency is versatile and can be used to aid any manifestation that's attempting to enact change or growth in your life.

- **528 Hz** – for love. This love frequency is one of the most popular and can be used for manifesting love, a relationship, or your soul mate.

- **639 Hz** – for building healthy interpersonal relationships. Use it if your manifestation involves your family, friends, or anything communication-based.

- **741 Hz** – for puzzle solving, creativity, and self-expression. This frequency aids with intuition and gets those creative juices flowing so you can finish your masterpiece or outsmart that problem that's been plaguing you.

- **852 Hz** – for spiritual reconnection. Use this frequency if you feel you've lost your connection with the universe. It will get you back into balance.

- **963 Hz** – for achieving the "perfect state." This highest frequency helps you let go of your earthly worries and fears and regain a deeply spiritual, almost childlike state of pure joy and hope.

DON'T LET
ANYTHING STAND
IN YOUR WAY

MANIFESTATION BLOCKS

Sometimes, you'll be manifesting and manifesting and manifesting for something to happen, and it just won't. It could be because there are manifestation blocks in your way. These are any obstacles that inhibit your manifestations, preventing you from utilizing the law of attraction effectively. Luckily, there are lots of things you can do about it. This section first discusses subconscious reprogramming, a tool for overcoming mental barriers, and then lists some of the most frequently occurring manifestation blocks, so that you will be better equipped to identify what's stopping your manifestations and to tackle these obstacles head-on.

SUBCONSCIOUS REPROGRAMMING

We all like staying in our comfort zone. It's, well, comfortable! And as it turns out, our brains, which are wired to regulate our bodies and keep everything balanced and in harmony, might be regulating us mentally as well. Our brains are more likely to accept and highlight experiences that reinforce our preexisting beliefs and situations, meaning that we are naturally more likely to make choices that keep us in our comfort zone. This is why most of us, at one point or another, have thought, "I'll never achieve this, so there's no point trying." But the good news is that you can change the way your brain is wired to make yourself think more positively about your goals and welcome change into your life. This is called subconscious reprogramming, and the following tips will assist you as you start training your subconscious mind to work *for* you and your goals, not against them.

Whenever you doubt yourself or the universe, give yourself permission to be happy in the present moment. We often fall into the trap of believing we'll only be happy once we've got that new job or lost this amount of weight. If this sounds like you, take five minutes each day to repeat to yourself, "I am happy, and I allow good things into my life." Over time, this will help retrain your subconscious into being content in the here and now, raising your energy's vibration and sending out positive vibes to the universe. You can't attract happiness into your life if you aren't already happy with what you have! To help with this, fill your daily routine with positive encouragement and reinforcement. Put sticky notes on your laptop saying, "You've got this!"; change your morning alarm to an upbeat, celebratory song; and only follow people on social media who spread joy and positivity. This will help reprogram your brain into a constant state of confidence and belief.

TIP: NIGHTTIME REPROGRAMMING

Our brains are in their most open and receptive state in those peaceful, drifting moments just before we fall asleep. This halfway state between waking and dreaming is the ideal time for influencing and altering our subconscious programming. But it's not easy to catch yourself as you fall asleep and start chanting positive affirmations—besides, this will just wake you up! Instead, take advantage of your brain's willingness to unlearn harmful thought patterns during this period by listening to subliminal recordings as you go to sleep. These often take the form of soothing music and other audio like rainfall or waves on a beach with positive affirmations "hidden" in the mix and can be found on YouTube or Spotify. Give them a try to see how much they help with your subconscious reprogramming.

TRUST THAT THE
UNIVERSE HAS A
BIGGER, WIDER,
DEEPER DREAM
FOR YOU THAN
YOU COULD
EVER IMAGINE
FOR YOURSELF.

OPRAH WINFREY

MANIFESTATION BLOCK ONE: DOUBTING THE PROCESS

Guess what? If you don't believe that manifestation works, then it won't! You have to truly believe that the universe has the power to give you what you want, or it simply won't happen. But that's easier said than done, especially if you're a first-time manifestor who hasn't yet had the chance to witness the power of manifestation. This is where positive affirmations can really help. Choose from one of these and repeat it to yourself whenever you catch yourself doubting the manifestation process:

- The universe is ready and willing to give me what I desire.

- The universe and I can work together to achieve anything.

- The universe has my back!

Writing down evidence of your manifestations will also help to solidify your belief in the process. For example, if you're manifesting money and your friend, unprompted, recommends her new bargain phone deal, write it down as evidence! Even if it's only small things, having a list like this will prove that the universe is making things happen.

MANIFESTATION BLOCK TWO: DOUBTING YOURSELF

Maybe you trust that the universe has the power to give you happiness, but you don't believe that you deserve it. "I'm not good enough"; "I always fail at everything"; "Why do I even bother..." If we believe that we won't achieve, then it hampers our progress and we're more likely to miss the mark. Overcoming self-doubt can be a long journey, so don't beat yourself up if you're not over it in a day; it's possible and achievable! Meditation, daily positive affirmations, and self-care routines are all tried-and-tested methods for boosting self-esteem and self-belief. Another technique you could try is a belief assessment. Sit quietly for five minutes. Reflect on what it is you desire, try to identify the beliefs you have that are holding you back, and then turn each belief on its head to create an alternative, self-affirming belief. Repeat each one to yourself five times. Do this regularly and you'll become a pro at challenging your limiting thoughts and doubts!

MANIFESTATION BLOCK THREE: BAD HABITS

This one is a bit of a catchall: bad habits are any number of smaller, day-to-day manifestation blocks that occur either during your manifestation sessions or throughout your day. You probably don't know you're doing them! Bad habits during manifestation practice might be things like keeping an untidy, stressful environment; forgetting to remove distractions; or negative self-talk during a session. But the way you behave throughout the rest of your daily life can also have an impact (positive or negative) on your manifestation. For example, if you neglect to carry out self-care like getting enough sleep or fresh air, you're telling the universe that you don't deserve to be looked after or given abundance. So if you're finding that your manifestations aren't coming easily, have a think about the habits and routines you've formed to see if there's anything you can improve on. But remember: you don't have to be absolutely perfect in order to manifest successfully, so don't beat yourself up.

MANIFESTATION BLOCK FOUR: OTHER PEOPLE

You may find that there is a minority of people—and they could be your friends, family, colleagues, or merely acquaintances—who seem to be trying their best to pull your vibrational frequency down. Perhaps it's what they say to you ("Do you really think that's a good idea?") or what they say about themselves ("I've stopped trying; I don't see the point."), but their negative energy is creeping up on you, and before you know it you're struggling to manifest! In most cases, these people intend no harm, so try your best to lift their energy (instead of letting them drag yours down) with positive chat, smiles, and cups of tea. In rarer cases, you may come to the difficult decision that you're better off without that person in your life, although this requires careful deliberation and a sensitive approach. Only you can know whether the relationship is working or whether your instincts are telling you to walk away.

MANIFESTATION BLOCK FIVE: WRONG TIMING

You've done everything right: you've banished your doubt, you've refined your habits and daily routine, and you've stopped listening to the naysayers. So why isn't your manifestation coming true *right now*? Well, it could be the timing. Rest assured, the universe *has* heard you and is willing to work with you, but sometimes the timing doesn't work out immediately. Say you've carried out all the steps to manifest your dream career and you're frustrated that nothing seems to be happening yet. But perhaps a position is going to become available at your ideal company—six months from now. Would you prefer to settle for something else or ride out those six months for the opportunity of a lifetime? It's hard to be patient, but it's exactly what you need to do—and in the meantime you can continue to put in the hard work. You don't know exactly what the universe has in store for you, or when it will happen, but it will absolutely be worth the wait!

YOU ARE
UNSTOPPABLE

CHAPTER FIVE:

MAKING IT HAPPEN

You've come a long way on your manifestation journey. You have a variety of visualization and scripting techniques at your disposal, and you have the confidence to tackle manifestation blocks when they occur. So what's next? This chapter covers the final two of the five main manifestation stages: taking action and expressing gratitude. Although they may seem like an afterthought, they are two of the most crucial steps for making your manifestations happen and keeping you motivated. The chapter also provides advice for keeping the momentum high as you manifest in the long term, so that manifestation can become an enduring part of your life.

TAKE ACTION

Manifestation is a collaboration between you and the universe. It wouldn't be reasonable to expect the universe to do all the heavy lifting while you sit back and wait for the results, so get ready for some serious work. For many, this is the most exciting phase of manifestation: a chance for you to get into your passions and begin making concrete progress toward your goals. The tips and advice in the following pages will help you stay motivated if you're feeling a bit overwhelmed and will help you avoid burnout and watch out for signs from the universe.

JUST ONE THING

As you begin the process of manifesting one of your goals, it's important to start working toward that goal *now*. Don't wait until your 5, 21, or 30 days of scripting are up! Taking action immediately makes you act more like the person you're going to be once you've achieved your goal, raising your vibrational frequency to match that of whatever you're trying to attract. You might think there's nothing you can do today to bring you closer to your goal, but there's *always* something, even if it's only tiny. For example, say you're manifesting owning your own business. You're probably not going to be able to launch your fully fledged business tomorrow, but you can research other businesses you'd like to emulate, come up with three ideas about how to market your product or service, or arrange a coffee date with a small-business owner you know. Just do one thing every day and it won't be long until you see plentiful results.

INTENTION JOURNAL

So you've chosen what to manifest, you've done your visualizing and scripting, gotten rid of your blocks, and now you're trying to put it into action. It's hard, isn't it? It's much easier to forget about your end goal, lose focus, and get caught up instead in the motions of everyday life. You might start to feel like you're stuck in an endless loop rather than progressing forward. Eventually, you'll wonder why change isn't happening in your life. But don't worry: here's one technique that will help you stay focused on the actions you need to take to achieve any goal you may have. It's called an intention journal. Writing down your intentions for each day, week, or month not only sends a clear message to the universe about what you want but also helps you identify and stick to an action plan for making your manifestations real, thus boosting your motivation for achieving both short-term and long-term goals.

Decide whether you want to keep your intention journal daily, weekly, or monthly and set aside 10 minutes at the very start or end of your day to fill it out. Make a short list of your intentions for that day, week, or month, making sure that they align with your manifestations. Three to five items is a good amount. Start each item with the words "I intend." You might want to make your intentions very specific ("I intend to run for 30 minutes today"), very broad ("I intend to be open to new ideas today"), or a mixture of the two. If you've chosen to fill out your intention journal weekly or monthly, make sure your intentions are suitable for the longer time frame. Fill out your journal regularly, and after a couple of months set aside some time to read back through and reflect on your intentions. How did you do? Are you closer to your goals? Doing this will help you form clearer intentions going forward.

WHEN
OPPORTUNITY
COMES
KNOCKING,
OPEN THE DOOR

GIVE YOURSELF A BREAK

When you're in the middle of a manifestation, and you're scripting or visualizing every day and working hard to make your manifestation a reality, it's easy to forget one of the most important things for manifestation (and life!): joy. Remember: keeping your vibrational frequency high is how you're going to attract good things from the universe. If you're stressed out, you're only going to manifest more stress into your life! So it's important to do something every day that makes you happy, purely for the joy of it. Whether it's a hobby like sports or crafts, meeting up with friends for a drink, or chilling out in front of the TV, ensure that you make time for yourself, without any additional goal or motive other than having fun. This will help keep your energy high, you'll be more relaxed, and, above all, happier.

ACT THE PART

A lot of manifestations aren't successful because people aren't thinking and acting as though they have already achieved their goal. They use language such as "I wish" or "I hope," and they're reluctant to change anything about their behavior or routines. It's no wonder that they struggle to raise their energy and attract what they want! So, as you manifest your goals, be sure to act the part. This can take many forms, but it's not about lying to yourself or others. If you ever feel like you're pretending to be something you're not, stop! This is a surefire way to lower your energy. But there's plenty you can do to start embodying the person you're going to be when you've reached your goal.

1. **Speech and language:** How would a person who has what you want speak? Would someone who has the perfect house you're trying to manifest go around bragging about it? Probably not. But they wouldn't complain about how awful it is, either.

2. Appearance: Don't worry; you don't have to go out and buy an entirely new wardrobe. But someone with the high-flying job you want might smile plenty, stand and walk confidently with their head held high, or wear the clothes they want without caring what others think.

3. Behavior: How would someone act if they had the amount of money you want to manifest? Would they avoid checking their bank balance because they're too scared? Would they be overly cautious about investing or being generous to others? No! And while it's not wise to throw your money away on foolish endeavors, burying it in the ground (metaphorically or literally) isn't going to attract abundance either.

GUT INSTINCTS

Getting out of your comfort zone can be tricky, but it's going to be necessary when you're working to achieve your goals. Luckily, there's a way of knowing when taking a leap of faith is the right thing to do. Call it gut instinct, intuition, or that little voice in your head, but when you just have a sense that you should make that decision, do that action, or take that risk, you should probably listen up and do it! It could be your own subconscious instincts, or a guiding voice from the universe, or a guardian angel, but they might know something you don't. Say you're manifesting a relationship and you just get a *feeling* that you should visit your favorite coffee shop today or send a message to one of your old school friends you haven't seen in years (or maybe a certain someone has started popping up in your dreams)—listen to your gut; who knows what amazing things could happen.

SIGNS FROM THE UNIVERSE

As you embark on the process of taking action toward your manifestation goals, remember to be on the lookout for signs from the universe that your manifestation is on its way. These signs might be in the form of the gut instincts discussed earlier, but they can also be external and material as well. And they might not always be what you expect, so it's a good idea to be open and receptive to opportunities that come your way—these could be the universe giving you a little nudge in the right direction! If you're manifesting a promotion at work, you might be expecting your boss to ask for a meeting. You might not be expecting a colleague to ask you to collaborate with them on a project—but this project could be just the opportunity to prove your worth. The universe sometimes works in slightly roundabout ways, so you've got to be ready to go with the flow.

ANGEL NUMBERS

One specific type of sign from the universe that you should be on the lookout for is angel numbers. These most often take the form of a series of repeating digits (like 333) that you'll suddenly start seeing everywhere. Perhaps you keep checking the time when it's exactly 3:33 p.m., your grocery total comes to $3.33, or you check your Instagram followers and there are precisely 333 of them. This is your angel number! First and foremost, angel numbers are a sign that the universe is listening to your manifestations and is willing to help you manifest your goals, but the different angel numbers have their own meanings as well. These can be varied and nuanced, but some basic meanings are set out here. It's also important to note that your angel number can change, especially if you've started a new manifestation or have changed direction. The universe might have new guidance for you.

- **111** – Remember to keep your thoughts and energy focused on your goals.

- **222** – Be present in the moment and find balance.

- **333** – Something is happening. Expect good news!

- **444** – You're on the right track. Keep going and follow your instincts.

- **555** – Change is coming, so be prepared for it.

- **666** – You need to make a change, shift your perspective, or return to focus.

- **777** – Give up control and take time to rest and relax.

- **888** – You've made good progress, so be grateful. An angelic pat on the back!

- **999** – Something needs to end. Let go of the past to make room for the future.

ACKNOWLEDGE AND BE GRATEFUL

Gratitude is one of the keys to successful manifestation. If you don't show gratitude for the things you already have, it's going to be difficult to convince the universe that you're ready for and worthy of additional abundance. So, once you've manifested something in your life, it's time to say thank you to the universe for giving you this blessing. The next few pages first explain the concept of a gratitude loop and then give a couple of different ideas for entering into this gratitude loop. An endless cycle of continued abundance is within your grasp!

GRATITUDE LOOP

When you express gratitude for everything that happens to you—small and big—you will find that your next manifestation will be easier, faster, or more successful. This is because continuing to be grateful sends out an enduring signal of positive energy to the universe, which will be returned to you due to the law of attraction. This is sometimes called a gratitude loop: an unlimited cycle of positive energy, created by your gratitude, that fuels your manifestations present and future. The more gratitude you express to the universe for giving you what you want, the more the universe will continue to listen to and answer your manifestations. Conversely, if the universe has helped you manifest something and you neglect to say thank you, the stream of positive energy will be broken and you might find it very difficult or even impossible to manifest anything else. This is why gratitude loops are so important!

GRATITUDE JOURNAL

The simplest way of entering and maintaining a gratitude loop for your manifestations is by keeping a daily gratitude journal. Writing down the good things that happen to you and visualizing and focusing on the emotions of gratitude each day will raise your energy's vibration, helping you enter into your gratitude loop and tap into the universe's overflowing abundance. Keeping a gratitude journal is easy and doesn't require much time, effort, or equipment. It can also be done even if you're yet to complete a manifestation—in fact, it's probably going to help! Your journal will help you to maintain a gratitude loop that will keep your energy in a high vibrational state, enabling you to manifest more effectively but also, crucially, allowing you to demonstrate to the universe that you are truly thankful for everything it has done for you.

Set aside 5 to 10 minutes at the end of your day for this method. Visualize five things that happened that day that you are grateful for. They might be related to your current manifestations—perhaps you got one step closer—or they might be other things, like something fun you did or a kindness someone showed you. Take a little while to visualize each event, remembering how you felt when they happened and how you feel to have these continued blessings in your life. Bask in the warmth of your gratitude for each item. Then, write down the five things you visualized (remember to start each one with "I am grateful for"). Repeat this each night—you might want to start a new journal dedicated to your gratitude affirmations, as they will build up quickly! Every so often, read your gratitude journal back, remember just how much you have to be grateful for, and take time to thank the universe again for the abundance it has given you.

ACKNOWLEDGING
THE GOOD THAT
YOU ALREADY
HAVE IN YOUR
LIFE IS THE
FOUNDATION FOR
ALL ABUNDANCE.

ECKHART TOLLE

PAY IT FORWARD

Another positive way of demonstrating your thanks to the universe is by paying it forward to other people. The universe has provided you with good things and now you have the opportunity to spread the goodness throughout your own little corner of the world. Paying it forward can come in many different shapes and sizes: perhaps you want to carry out some random acts of kindness like paying for the next person's order at the coffee shop; doing something nice for a friend or loved one, like taking them out for a fun trip; or simply handing out compliments and encouragement to everyone you speak to. As well as making these people's days, you'll reap plenty of benefits: fulfillment, joy, and raised energy, just to name a few. Demonstrate to the universe that you truly appreciate the good things it has given you, so much so that you want to share the abundance with as many others as you can.

ASK FOR WHAT
YOU WANT—THEN
GO GET IT!

KEEP IT FRESH

If you've been manifesting for a while, you might find that it starts to lose its sparkle. You're no longer as excited to do your visualization or scripting each day, and you're noticing that you're not getting the results you were experiencing when you first started. This is totally normal. No one finds it easy to maintain a super-high vibrational frequency 100 percent of the time. That's when the following tips come in handy. There are a couple of ideas you can use if you feel like you're getting bogged down with your manifesting, so you can start to sparkle again.

BACK TO BASICS

We're all human. Keeping up your high energy and positive mindset at all times when you've been manifesting for a while is a big challenge, especially when you've been going through a rough patch or are experiencing challenges and adversity. If you feel like you're stuck in a rut or that your manifestations just aren't working the way they used to, try going back to basics. Reread the earlier chapters of this book, brush up on the essentials, and rediscover a technique or two that you might think you've moved beyond. You'll be reminded of the importance of the core manifestation elements, and trying a less complex method is ideal if you're going through a stressful period. Going back to the simple, bare bones of manifestation might be just what you need to clear your mind and realign your focus. Think of it like a spring clean for your energy!

MIX IT UP

Another thing to try if you're stuck in a manifestation rut is the simple act of switching up your routine. While it is true that keeping a regular daily manifestation routine can be hugely beneficial for your vibration and focus, after awhile, repeating the same thing day in, day out will get stale, especially if you're always sticking to the same manifestation method. You'll switch to autopilot, possibly without even noticing, and your vibrational frequency will start to drop. So it's worth changing up your routine and trying out new techniques in your manifestation sessions every so often. If you usually stick to visualization, why not try out a scripting technique—or vice versa. You might also want to consider adding or switching up other practices, such as daily morning affirmations, a new meditation method, or a fresh vision board, to keep it interesting. You never want your manifesting to become a chore!

IT'S NOT MAGIC

It's important to remember that manifestation isn't magic. It's not a modern-day fairy godmother that will make all your wildest dreams come true with a wave of her magic wand. It takes a lot of continued focus and effort from you. So if your manifestations just aren't working out the way you want, take heart. This isn't always going to be easy! Try taking a break, mixing up your routine, or trying out a relaxing activity to help get you back into the right headspace. Don't listen to anyone trying to tell you that you're not manifesting hard enough or you don't want it enough. The only person who knows what you want and what works for you is *you*. And, above all, be patient. Manifestation can't solve all your problems instantly. But if you're willing to wait, and work for it in the meantime, manifestation can become your most valued tool on the path to success.

FIGHT AND
PUSH HARDER
FOR WHAT YOU
BELIEVE IN...
YOU ARE MUCH
STRONGER THAN
YOU THINK.

LADY GAGA

CONCLUSION

Manifestation is powerful and empowering. Learning about the secrets of manifestation and implementing them in your life is an incredible journey toward joy, achievement, and self-actualization—a journey that started with the earliest New Thought figures who first wrote about the astonishing law of attraction and continues, now, with you. Using what you have learned in this book, you are capable of amazing things, as long as you're committed and prepared to collaborate with the universe. And while manifestation has its highs (and plenty of them), you're also going to come up against challenges that test your belief, willpower, confidence, and patience. You've just got to keep pushing forward—and go easy on yourself if you falter. Nobody's perfect! And remember, anything that's worth having is not going to be straightforward or easy to get, but it will be 100 percent worth it in the end, when you've achieved your most longed-for goals and you're basking in that sweet sense of accomplishment, pride, and joy. The power to shape the life you want rests ultimately with *you*.

RESOURCES

BOOKS

Bernstein, Gabrielle *Super Attractor* (2019, Hay House)

Byrne, Rhonda *The Secret* (2006, Beyond Words)

Byrne, Rhonda *How the Secret Changed My Life* (2016, Simon & Schuster)

Coelho, Paulo *The Alchemist* (1993, HarperTorch)

Hicks, Esther and Hicks, Jerry *Ask and It Is Given* (2004, Hay House)

Hill, Napoleon *Think and Grow Rich* (1937, The Ralston Society)

King, Vex *Good Vibes, Good Life* (2018, Hay House)

Redfield, James *The Celestine Prophecy* (1993, Satori Publishing)

Tolle, Eckhart *The Power of Now* (1997, Namaste Publishing)

Wattles, Wallace Delois *The Science of Getting Rich* (1910, Elizabeth Towne Company)

WEBSITES

www.gabbybernstein.com – for manifestation inspiration

www.oprahdaily.com – for positive thinking and good vibes

www.thelawofattraction.com – for the history and theory of manifestation

www.themanifestationcollective.co – for manifestation tips and advice

AUDIO AND VIDEO

Aaron Doughty (YouTube channel)
Dear Gabby (podcast by Gabby Bernstein)
Leeor Alexandra (YouTube channel)
The Secret (2006 film)